Colorful Celia

Colorful Celia

The DaVinci of Appalachia

Sarah Lewis

gatekeeper press™
Columbus, OH

Colorful Celia: The DaVinci of Appalachia

Published by Gatekeeper Press
2167 Stringtown Rd, Suite 109
Columbus, OH 43123-2989
www.GatekeeperPress.com

Library of Congress Control Number: 2022934704

ISBN (hardcover): 9781662926785
ISBN (paperback): 9781662926792
eISBN: 9781662926808

This book is dedicated to the memory of my dear ol' dad who taught me to draw and to dare.

"Hey sweetie, come here and sit for a minute please and thank you."

"What is it, Mom?"

"I want to tell you a story about your great-great-grandmother, Celia."

"Aww, Mom do I have to?"

"Oh, shush it and come sit. Now because Celia's family has Irish heritage, her grandkids called her Mammy which is what the Irish call their mothers; But according to Aunt Ann, it is how everyone referred to Celia. So, we will too. Celia is from Appalachia."

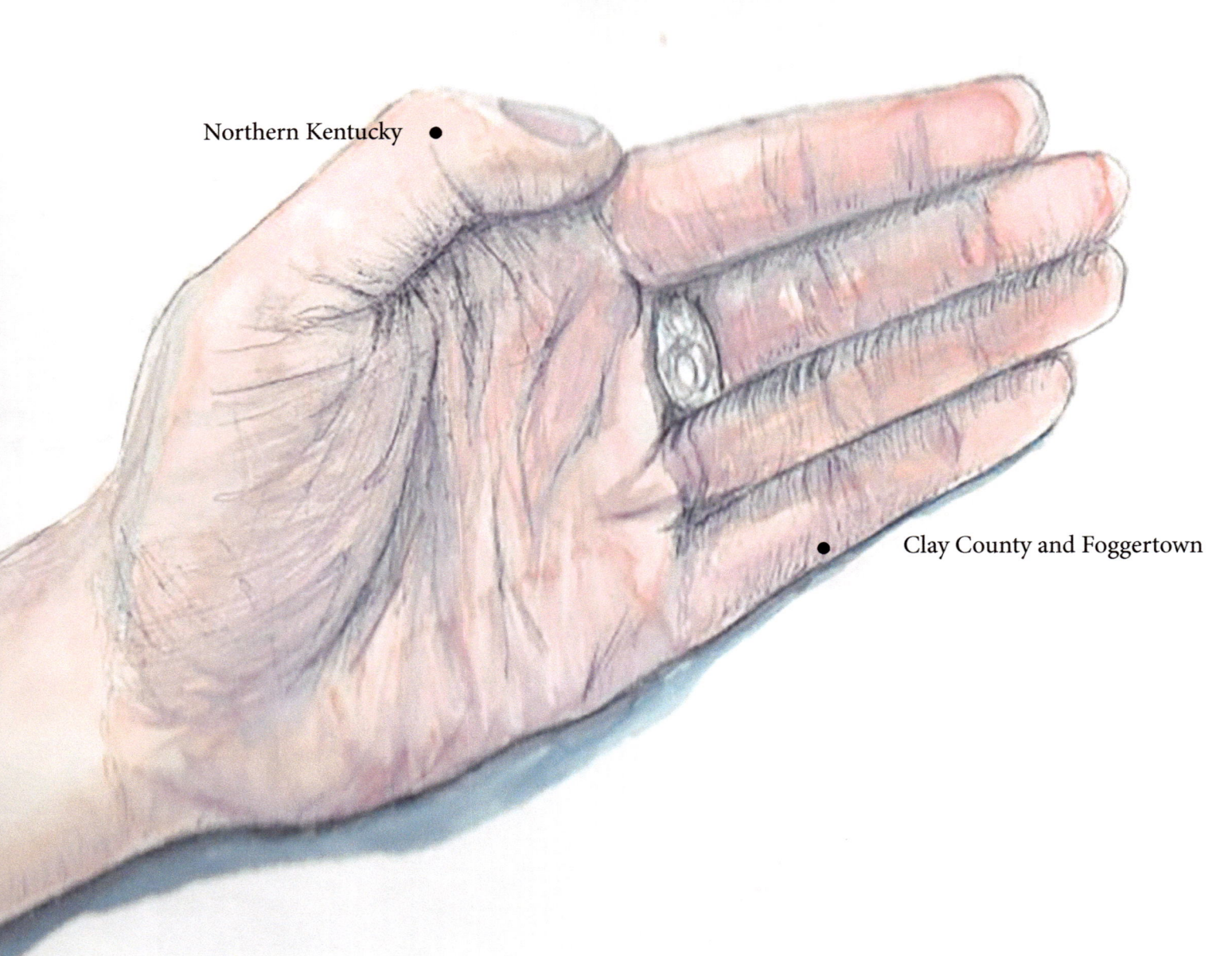

Northern Kentucky

Clay County and Foggertown

"Mom, where's Appaplacia?"

"You mean, *Appalachia*? Here. If you look at the palm of your hand and pretend it is Kentucky, we are at the northern part by your thumb and Appalachia is at the bottom right part of your palm. That's where Clay County is. Celia lived at a beautiful farm there by Red Bird River."

"Celia's mom stayed at home and did all the chores like laundry, cooking, cleaning, and Celia was expected to do the same. However, nature had other plans. She was given a creative gift of painting. This was unusual in the mountains of Kentucky during this time, because women worked very hard cleaning, cooking, raising the kids, taking care of the farm animals, and working the land with their husbands... women didn't paint, didn't have time to."

"Mom, giwls should be allowed to paint. Like just give them some paints, it's OK guys."

"I agree sweet pea! Your great aunt Ann told me a story about when Mammy Celia was little. She would always look up at the sky fascinated by its different moods, and whenever her mother observed her doing this would exclaim, 'Oh Lawd, there's somethin' wrong with this child!'. Later, when Celia was eighty-eight years old, a newspaperman from *The Louisville Courier* came to interview her about her art and she recalled with a smile, 'Ever' time mother would catch me drawin', she'd say it was laziness. She thought I was tryin' to get out of work.'

"And you know what's interesting, girlie?"

"What Mom?"

"You and I both stare at the sky in the same way-I am always fascinated by the clouds, and I think about what kind of brush stroke or paint hue I would use to capture its particular mood-And we have our head in the clouds like Celia. You know, she even still climbed trees at eighty-five years old?!?"

"Mom?"

"Yes?"

"I weally like hewr.

"Schools were different back then too. Kids of all ages went to a one-room schoolhouse."

"I know, Mom, you've told me this before."

"Oh, hush it sassafras. Here's a newspaper clipping of Celia's class in 1900 when she was about twelve years old-she's smiling and making an x shape with her arms across her chest when no one else is-you can tell even from this picture that your great grandma was a little bit different."

"Ok, let's see. . . In the 1920s Celia married Grover Cleveland Markum."

"Ha ha ha, is that his weal name?!"

"Unfortunately."

"Anyways, Grover bought Mammy Celia her first set of oil paints off a drunken artist on the side of a road and that was the beginning of a lifetime of creativity that would lead to one newspaperman calling her 'Grandma Moses of the Mountains' in 1964. She painted lots of landscapes and horses. It's amazing that she had the time given that she had NINE children. Somehow, she still made room for her art."

"My dad once told me, when he was little, he used to sit at Celia's feet in her kitchen-mesmerized while watching her cook, can, and paint simultaneously. I asked him, 'What did she paint? He said, 'Whatever was out her window that day.'"

"Wow! She's perdy amazing."

"A print of her most famous painting hangs in the Frontier Nursing Service Bed and Breakfast. Your great-great-grandmother was friends with the founder of the Frontier Nursing Service, Mary Breckinridge. Mary moved to Kentucky with various other British and Scottish midwives to give medical care to pregnant women, mothers, and children in Appalachia because there were no doctors for two counties Celia painted the frontier nurses crossing the Red Bird River on horseback while it was snowing because these nurse midwives really would have to cross that river to get to their patients no matter the weather."

"In addition to painting and sewing, Mammy Celia was also featured in a newspaper in 1941 for her training program for the National Youth Association. -Many girls and boys in Appalachia were very underweight because they weren't getting the nourishment their bodies needed for they didn't know how to farm the land to get the most nutrients. -So, Celia had a boot camp of sorts, for girls who wanted to learn how to farm.

"Celia recalled, 'One girl, who had such a bad case of rickets that she couldn't walk a city block without falling three or four times, gained about twenty pounds after having been here about a year and became as strong as any girl we had.'"

"Isn't that so amazing girlie? Mammy Celia was so creative artistically, but also, she was creative in how to help people. -I think the biggest thing she has taught me is to give myself permission to make room for art like she did."

"Mom? I know I got my gift of awt from Grandma Celia. . . and I got my sassy from hewr too."

CPSIA information can be obtained
at www.ICGtesting.com
Printed in the USA
LVHW011931100723

752030LV00004B/167